Crypto Investing for Beginners

Build a Long-Term Portfolio, Avoid Rookie Mistakes, and Start Growing Wealth Today

By Joe Correa

Published by Live Stronger Faster

This book is for educational and informational purposes only. The author and publisher are not engaged in rendering legal, financial, or other professional advice. Readers should consult a qualified professional before making any financial decisions.

First Edition

Table of Contents

Introduction to Crypto Investing for Beginners.......... 5

Chapter 1: Why Invest in Crypto?.......... 8

Chapter 2: Setting Up for Success — Mindset, Risk, and Planning.......... 15

Chapter 3: The Top Cryptocurrencies to Know and Why.......... 22

Chapter 4: Building Your First Crypto Portfolio — Allocations, Tools, and Timing.......... 31

Chapter 5: Storing and Securing Your Crypto — Wallets, Keys, and Safety Practices.......... 39

Chapter 6: Investing Strategies: Timing the Market, HODLing, and Taking Profits.......... 47

Chapter 7: Staking, Yield Farming, and Earning Passive Income with Crypto.......... 54

Chapter 8: Crypto Taxes, Reporting, and Legal Basics.......... 61

Chapter 9: Avoiding Scams, Mistakes, and Emotional Investing Traps. 69

Chapter 10: Creating Your Long-Term Crypto Wealth Plan.......... 77

Epilogue: Your Journey Begins Now.......... 85

Introduction to Crypto Investing for Beginners

Cryptocurrency investing has evolved from a niche curiosity into a global financial movement, offering everyday people an opportunity to build real wealth. If you're holding this book in your hands, it means you're ready to take that leap—from observer to investor. And you've made the right choice, because timing matters. We're still early in this revolution. While the markets have gone through booms and busts, just like any new asset class, the underlying adoption curve continues to grow. Those who learn the right principles now will be in the best position to profit long-term.

This book is not just a crash course on which coins to buy. It's a mindset shift. Here, you'll learn how to think like an investor—not a gambler, not a speculator, and certainly not someone who's simply chasing the next viral token. You'll learn how to evaluate coins based on fundamentals, how to understand risk and reward, and how to protect your capital through diversification, cold storage, and security. Investing in crypto is about more than just buying Bitcoin or Ethereum; it's about building a solid foundation that can grow with the future of the digital economy.

We'll start with the basics: what it means to invest in

cryptocurrency and why it's different from investing in traditional assets like stocks or real estate. Then, we'll cover how to identify strong projects, what metrics to look at, and how to avoid scams that prey on beginners. From there, we'll walk through creating a starter portfolio—complete with asset allocation strategies, risk management techniques, and dollar-cost averaging (DCA) plans. You'll even learn how to recognize market cycles, handle FOMO (Fear of Missing Out), and develop the discipline that separates long-term winners from short-term losers.

One of the biggest mistakes new investors make is treating crypto like a lottery ticket. They dump their money into whatever's trending on social media, expecting overnight returns. But real investing is about patience, education, and compounding over time. The good news? You don't need to be a genius or a tech expert. You just need to follow proven principles, use the right tools, and keep your emotions in check.

By the time you finish this book, you'll have a clear action plan for building your own crypto portfolio—whether you're starting with $50 or $50,000. You'll know how to evaluate projects, understand tokenomics, store your crypto safely, and decide when to buy, hold, or sell. You'll be armed with the confidence to participate in this exciting new asset class without falling into the traps that so many others do.

Investing in crypto is one of the most exciting opportunities of our generation. But it's also one of the most misunderstood. Let this book be your guide. Let it be the blueprint you come back to whenever you're unsure. And most of all, let it be your launchpad toward building real, lasting wealth in the digital age.

Let's get started.

Chapter 1: Why Invest in Crypto?

Cryptocurrency has evolved into one of the most dynamic investment opportunities of our time. But many beginners still wonder—why invest in crypto at all? What makes this asset class so appealing, and how does it compare to traditional investments like stocks, bonds, or real estate? The answer lies in a combination of innovation, accessibility, growth potential, and the chance to be early in a generational shift in finance and technology.

At its core, investing in crypto offers exposure to a decentralized future—one where financial power is distributed, not controlled by a single government or bank. This decentralization is not just a buzzword; it represents a fundamental shift in how value is created, transferred, and stored. Cryptocurrencies like Bitcoin introduced the world to the idea of peer-to-peer digital money that operates independently of traditional financial systems. Ethereum went a step further by allowing developers to build decentralized applications, ushering in new possibilities in finance, gaming, data storage, and more. As innovation in this space continues, crypto presents an opportunity to invest in the infrastructure of the future.

Another reason to consider crypto is its asymmetric risk-reward profile. While highly volatile, cryptocurrencies have delivered exponential returns for early adopters. In many traditional investments, the potential upside is often capped—stocks may grow 8–10% per year, and real estate might appreciate modestly over time. But in crypto, it's not uncommon for well-researched investments to double, triple, or even 10x within a few years—especially when you enter before mass adoption occurs. This doesn't mean you should bet your life savings, but even a small, calculated allocation to crypto can significantly impact your overall portfolio returns.

Accessibility is another major factor. You don't need a brokerage account, thousands of dollars, or a Wall Street connection to begin investing in crypto. With just a smartphone and internet connection, anyone in the world can participate. This is especially empowering for people in developing countries or underbanked communities, where traditional banking systems may be inefficient, corrupt, or completely inaccessible. Crypto offers a level playing field—everyone has the same tools, the same market access, and the same information if they're willing to learn.

Inflation protection is also a growing reason people are turning to crypto. Governments around the world have printed trillions of dollars in recent years, leading to currency devaluation and rising prices. In contrast, Bitcoin is hard-coded to have a fixed supply—only 21 million will ever exist. This makes it an appealing hedge against inflation, much like digital gold. As trust in fiat currencies continues to erode, crypto provides a decentralized alternative that cannot be manipulated by a central authority. This kind of monetary policy transparency is rare in global finance and a key part of the crypto narrative.

Crypto is also attractive to those who want to align their investments with emerging technology trends. Just as investors once bought into the internet, smartphones, and social media platforms before they exploded in value, today's crypto investors are backing projects that could define the future of finance, identity, ownership, and digital interaction. NFTs, DeFi (decentralized finance), Web3, and tokenization are just a few areas creating new markets and opportunities. Investing in crypto is like buying into the internet before Google, Facebook, or Amazon went public—except now, the barrier to entry is even lower.

Of course, crypto is not without risks. Price volatility is extreme. Scams are common. Regulation is still evolving. But this is precisely why education is so critical. Investors who approach this space with the right mindset—treating it as a long-term investment, diversifying wisely, and doing deep research—have a massive advantage over those who follow hype and speculation. Your goal should be to survive the volatility, not chase every pump and dump.

Crypto investing also comes with a powerful psychological benefit: sovereignty. When you own crypto, you hold your own keys, your own wealth, your own financial future. You're not dependent on a third-party custodian. You're not at the mercy of a bank freeze, a government policy change, or a market shutdown. For many, this level of financial freedom is priceless. It's a return to the core idea of money being a tool for independence—not dependence.

In summary, the reasons to invest in crypto are as much about the future as they are about the present. You're not just chasing gains—you're participating in a movement. A movement that's redefining money, trust, ownership, and access. Whether your goal is to grow wealth, diversify assets, or be part of something revolutionary, cryptocurrency offers a unique and powerful investment vehicle—one that rewards those who take the time to understand it and play the long game.

In the next chapter, we'll dive into the foundational steps to prepare yourself as a crypto investor—setting goals, understanding your risk profile, and choosing the right mindset for success.

Jason's story

It started with a simple question: "What if I miss this again?" Jason sat at his kitchen table, the morning sun creeping in through half-drawn blinds, his coffee untouched and cooling fast. He had just finished reading an article about a cryptocurrency called Solana that had increased 3,000% in value over the last year. His mind was racing—not because of greed, but because of regret. Years earlier, a friend had told him to buy Bitcoin when it was just under $1,000. He didn't. The idea seemed ridiculous then. Now, he couldn't stop thinking about how different his life would be if he had just invested a little. Not everything. Just something.

Jason wasn't a financial expert or a tech geek. He was a schoolteacher, disciplined in his budgeting and conservative with his savings. But something about this crypto movement felt different. It wasn't just about money anymore—it was about being part of a change. He watched his students talk about digital wallets and NFTs with more excitement than they ever showed for textbooks. He realized the world was moving forward whether he caught up or not.

That night, Jason opened his laptop, heart pounding like he

was doing something illegal. He searched for "how to invest in crypto safely." Terms like "decentralized," "blockchain," "cold storage," and "tokenomics" popped up. He didn't understand most of them, but he was determined to learn. He found beginner videos, read forums, listened to podcasts. It wasn't about chasing the next meme coin—it was about understanding what this movement represented. And it represented freedom.

Over the next few weeks, Jason learned that Bitcoin wasn't just a speculative asset; it was a digital store of value, a hedge against inflation. He learned that Ethereum wasn't just another coin—it was a platform where developers were building decentralized applications to solve real-world problems. He learned that crypto, for all its noise and hype, was a toolbox—one that offered transparency, sovereignty, and access to anyone with an internet connection. For someone like him, who had spent his life playing it safe and feeling like the financial world was a gated community, it felt empowering.

But he also learned about the risks. He read horror stories of people losing everything by clicking phishing links or investing in scam tokens. He read about people who bet their life savings, only to sell in a panic during market crashes. That wasn't going to be him. Jason created a plan—slow, methodical, and grounded. He decided to start with $50 a week. Enough to matter, but not enough to wreck him. He chose a mix of coins—some stable, some promising—and set up two-factor authentication on all his accounts. He stored his long-term holdings on a hardware wallet and kept a journal of his decisions and lessons learned.

Months passed. His portfolio went up, then down, then up again. But Jason didn't panic. He reminded himself of the reason he started—not to get rich quick, but to position himself for the long-term shift in how the world handled money and value. He started sharing what he learned with his colleagues, some of whom were still skeptical, some of whom became curious.

One day, a parent stopped him after school and asked, "Mr. Jason, my son says you helped him learn about investing in crypto. Is that true?" Jason smiled and nodded. The parent shook his hand and said, "Thank you. You've helped him think about his future differently."

Jason realized then that this wasn't just about charts, wallets, or profits. It was about unlocking something inside people—the courage to participate in a system that didn't require permission, the confidence to learn something new, and the patience to grow something valuable.

He wasn't chasing Lamborghinis or trying to time the market anymore. He was investing in knowledge, resilience, and the belief that ordinary people could take part in an extraordinary transformation. And for Jason, that was the greatest return on investment he could ever hope for.

Chapter 2: Setting Up for Success — Mindset, Risk, and Planning

Before you invest your first dollar into cryptocurrency, it's critical to establish a solid foundation—starting with your mindset, your risk tolerance, and your investment plan. Too many beginners jump into the market with dreams of overnight riches, only to crash emotionally and financially during their first correction. The truth is, successful crypto investing is not about picking the perfect coin or timing the market perfectly—it's about preparing your mindset, managing your emotions, and having a strategy you can stick to in any market condition.

Let's begin with mindset. The crypto space is volatile, unpredictable, and emotionally intense. You will see your portfolio swing up and down—sometimes by 10% or more in a single day. If your mindset is based on fear or greed, you'll end up making impulsive decisions: panic-selling at the bottom or buying in at the peak. A healthy mindset understands that investing is a long-term journey. You must think in years, not days. View short-term dips as opportunities, not disasters. Focus on learning, not just earning. Treat every experience—good or bad—as a lesson that brings you closer to mastery.

Next is understanding your personal risk tolerance. Everyone talks about "high risk, high reward," but very few truly understand what risk means. Risk tolerance is your ability and willingness to endure losses—both financially and emotionally—without abandoning your strategy. If you lose sleep when your investment drops 20%, you may be overexposed. Crypto is not one-size-fits-all. Some people may be comfortable with 20% of their net worth in crypto. Others may only be okay with 2%. Both are valid. What matters is aligning your exposure with your comfort level so you can stay in the game long enough to win.

Once you've clarified your mindset and risk profile, the next step is to create an investment plan. Start by identifying your goals. Are you investing for retirement, financial freedom, or just to learn? How much are you willing to invest each week or month? Will you use a lump sum or dollar-cost averaging (DCA)? How long are you willing to hold your investments—5 years, 10 years, or more? These questions will help you create a roadmap and protect you from the chaos of daily price action. Without a plan, it's easy to chase hype and abandon logic.

Diversification is another key principle. Don't put all your money into one coin—no matter how confident you are. The crypto market moves fast, and even strong projects can crash or stall. A smart strategy is to build a diversified portfolio that includes a mix of large-cap coins (like Bitcoin and Ethereum), mid-cap projects with strong fundamentals, and a small allocation to high-risk, high-reward tokens. This balance gives you exposure to upside potential while managing downside risk.

It's also important to understand liquidity and accessibility. You should never invest money you can't afford to lose or lock away for years. Emergencies happen. Bills need to be paid. That's why you should have a solid emergency fund before going deep into crypto. This ensures you're not forced to sell your holdings at a loss when life throws you a curveball. Investing in crypto should complement your financial life, not complicate it.

Planning also includes security. Many new investors lose their funds not because of bad investments, but because of bad security. Set up two-factor authentication (2FA) on all accounts. Use strong, unique passwords. Keep your recovery phrases offline and secure. If you use a hardware wallet, learn how to back it up and store it properly. If you use a centralized exchange, understand the risks of custodial wallets. A few hours of security prep can save you from devastating losses later.

Lastly, give yourself permission to evolve. Your strategy today may not be your strategy next year—and that's okay. As you learn more, your risk tolerance, goals, and portfolio structure may change. What's important is staying consistent in your process, continuing your education, and making decisions based on logic—not emotion.

In crypto, the greatest asset you have is not the coins you hold—it's the mindset and discipline you bring to the table. The market will always test you. Your preparation, patience, and planning are what will set you apart from the masses. With the right foundation in place, you're ready to start building a portfolio that reflects your goals, your beliefs, and your future.

In the next chapter, we'll explore the most important cryptocurrencies you should consider for your portfolio and how to evaluate their long-term potential.

How Amanda overcame her crypto trading nerves

Amanda had always been the type to plan everything. She made grocery lists for the week, color-coded her calendar, and triple-checked her retirement contributions every January. So, when she became curious about cryptocurrency, her instinct wasn't to jump in—it was to build a framework. She'd seen enough friends post screenshots of their wild gains and equally wild losses to know that crypto wasn't something to take lightly.

One evening, after reading yet another article about the growing adoption of blockchain in finance and tech, she decided to explore it seriously. But not emotionally. She wasn't going to gamble. She wanted to invest. With purpose. With discipline.

Her first step was to check her mindset. Amanda had a healthy relationship with money—she viewed it as a tool, not a status symbol. Still, the volatility of crypto made her nervous. She had seen a friend invest $10,000 in a hot altcoin and lose half of it in two weeks. That wasn't going to be her. She made a promise to herself: she wouldn't chase anything she didn't understand. She'd build a plan, and she'd stick to it.

Amanda started watching videos from long-term crypto investors, not just influencers pushing the next big token. She read books, joined online forums, and followed educational accounts on social media. One message echoed across them all: volatility is normal, and mindset is everything. She learned that investing wasn't about being right every time—it was about surviving long enough for your good decisions to pay off.

Next, Amanda assessed her risk tolerance. She wasn't rich, but she was stable. She had a six-month emergency fund, no consumer debt, and a solid 401(k). Crypto, she decided, would be her “innovation allocation”—a portion of her portfolio she was willing to let ride the highs and lows for the next 5–10 years. After careful consideration, she chose to allocate 5% of her investable assets to crypto. That felt ambitious enough to matter, but safe enough to sleep at night.

Then came the planning. Amanda didn’t want to time the market. She’d read about dollar-cost averaging—investing a fixed amount on a consistent schedule—and it made perfect sense. She set up a recurring buy of $200 every two weeks, split between Bitcoin, Ethereum, and a small-cap project she believed in after weeks of research. She journaled her decision-making process so she could review it later, and even printed out her plan and taped it inside her desk drawer as a reminder: "Stick to the process."

She also diversified her approach. Amanda didn’t just buy coins because they were popular. She looked at utility, market cap, development teams, community engagement, and tokenomics. If a project didn’t have a real-world use case or a clear reason to exist, she passed. Her portfolio was 70% Bitcoin and Ethereum, 20% in top-20 altcoins, and 10% in carefully chosen long shots. She didn’t expect every one to win—but she expected her winners to outweigh her losers over time.

Security was another focus. Amanda had always been cautious online, but crypto required another level. She researched cold wallets and purchased a hardware wallet for her long-term holdings. She enabled 2FA on all exchange accounts, used password managers, and stored her recovery phrases in a fireproof safe. She even did practice runs: testing how to recover her wallet if something went wrong. It felt empowering to take control of her financial sovereignty.

The biggest change, however, was internal. Amanda noticed she no longer panicked when prices dropped. When the market dipped 20% one month, her coworkers were stressing out—but Amanda calmly bought her usual $200 and walked away. Her confidence didn't come from luck. It came from preparation. She wasn't reacting to headlines—she was following her plan.

Months turned into a year. Her portfolio grew, then fell, then recovered. But her mindset, her risk discipline, and her planning never wavered. She began mentoring friends and even gave a presentation at her local community center titled "Crypto Without Chaos: Investing with Strategy." People listened. Some thanked her. And in those moments, she realized that the real power of crypto wasn't just the tech—it was the personal transformation it sparked in those who approached it with intention.

Amanda hadn't become rich overnight. But she had become something more valuable: a confident investor, capable of managing risk, embracing uncertainty, and creating a plan for the future. In a world of speculation, she had chosen structure. And it made all the difference.

Chapter 3: The Top Cryptocurrencies to Know and Why

Understanding which cryptocurrencies to invest in starts with understanding what they actually do and why they matter. The crypto world is filled with thousands of coins, but not all of them are worth your attention—or your money. In this chapter, we'll focus on the most important cryptocurrencies every beginner should know, and more importantly, *why* these projects are foundational to the future of blockchain and Web3.

Let's begin with **Bitcoin (BTC)**. Often referred to as digital gold, Bitcoin is the original cryptocurrency and the most widely recognized. It was created in 2009 by an anonymous figure named Satoshi Nakamoto, and its primary purpose is to serve as a decentralized, peer-to-peer form of digital money. But what makes Bitcoin truly revolutionary is its scarcity—there will only ever be 21 million BTC. This hard cap makes it an attractive store of value, especially in an era where central banks are printing more fiat currency than ever before. For many investors, Bitcoin is the first and most essential crypto holding, offering a secure, inflation-resistant foundation for any portfolio.

Next is **Ethereum (ETH)**, often called the world computer. While Bitcoin is focused on storing and transferring value, Ethereum is a programmable blockchain, allowing developers to build smart contracts and decentralized applications (dApps). Think of Ethereum as a platform rather than a currency. It powers entire ecosystems of decentralized finance (DeFi), NFTs, DAOs, and more. As a result, its utility goes far beyond speculation. Ethereum is in the process of transitioning to a more energy-efficient consensus model called proof-of-stake (via Ethereum 2.0), which aims to improve scalability and sustainability. For those interested in the broader future of Web3, Ethereum is a must-have.

Solana (SOL) is another standout project, known for its high-speed and low-cost transactions. While Ethereum has struggled with congestion and high gas fees, Solana offers a scalable alternative that's attracted developers building everything from NFT marketplaces to DeFi protocols. Though still relatively young, Solana's growing ecosystem and technical strengths make it a potential long-term winner—though it comes with more volatility and risk than more established coins like Bitcoin or Ethereum.

Chainlink (LINK) is a project that focuses on bridging the real world with the blockchain. It does this through decentralized oracles—systems that bring off-chain data onto the blockchain. For example, a smart contract for a decentralized insurance platform might need real-world weather data to execute. Chainlink provides that data securely and reliably. As more real-world use cases for blockchain emerge, Chainlink's importance will likely grow. It's not flashy, but it plays a critical behind-the-scenes role.

Polygon (MATIC) is a scaling solution for Ethereum that aims to make transactions faster and cheaper. It provides the infrastructure for developers to build dApps that benefit from Ethereum's security while offering better performance and affordability. Polygon has become one of the most widely adopted scaling platforms, making it an attractive choice for investors who believe in Ethereum but want exposure to projects improving its efficiency.

Other noteworthy coins include **Cardano (ADA)**, which focuses on academic research and peer-reviewed development to build a sustainable and scalable blockchain; **Avalanche (AVAX)**, another high-speed smart contract platform; and **Cosmos (ATOM)**, which enables different blockchains to communicate and share data. These projects each bring something unique to the crypto space and are worth researching further.

It's important to note that not all top-100 coins are good investments. Many are driven by hype and short-term trends. As a beginner, your focus should be on quality over quantity. Choose projects with real utility, strong development teams, active communities, and long-term roadmaps. Don't be swayed by price alone—a low-cost coin doesn't mean it has more room to grow. Look at market capitalization, adoption, partnerships, and the problem the coin is trying to solve.

To evaluate a cryptocurrency, ask these questions:

- What problem does it solve?
- Does it have a working product or just a whitepaper?
- Who's on the development team?
- What does its roadmap look like?
- Is it decentralized and secure?
- What is the tokenomics—how are tokens distributed and used?
- How active is its community and developer base?

A strong investment isn't just about potential—it's about durability. The coins mentioned above have survived multiple market cycles, indicating they're not just passing trends. Start by learning and investing in the top few, then gradually expand your exposure as your understanding deepens.

In the next chapter, we'll walk through how to build a beginner-friendly crypto portfolio using these top coins and others that meet your investment criteria.

Now, let's talk about Diego

Diego was a curious soul. He had spent most of his twenties traveling, writing blog posts, and working remote gigs just to make enough to live in places where the cost of living was low and the internet was fast. But as he neared thirty, he felt a tug—an urge to plant financial roots, to grow something that didn't require him to trade time for money. One night, while couch-surfing in Lisbon, he found himself deep into a podcast about Bitcoin and its role as digital gold. The host spoke with clarity, not hype, and something about it sparked Diego's curiosity in a new way.

He decided it was time to take crypto seriously—but this time, not just as a headline chaser or a FOMO-driven buyer. He wanted to understand the actual coins, their purpose, and their long-term potential. He pulled out his journal, made a fresh page titled "Crypto: What's Real and What's Noise," and began his research.

First, he dug into Bitcoin. The more he read, the more he appreciated its simplicity and power. It wasn't flashy. It didn't promise smart contracts or decentralized finance. It was digital scarcity, backed by a network of miners spread across the globe. No central authority. No inflation beyond the predetermined limit. Bitcoin, he realized, was less like a tech stock and more like a philosophy—about sovereignty, about value, and about time. He decided that his portfolio would always have Bitcoin at its core, no matter what.

Next, he explored Ethereum. At first, it overwhelmed him. There were dApps, smart contracts, DeFi platforms, NFTs, gas fees, and staking—all woven into this open-source ecosystem. But the more he watched videos and read developer blogs, the clearer it became: Ethereum was like an app store for the blockchain. Developers built on it. Entrepreneurs launched companies on it. Artists minted digital creations. Ethereum wasn't just another coin—it was a digital economy in motion. Diego saw the parallels between Ethereum today and the early days of the internet, and he knew he wanted a piece of it.

But Ethereum wasn't perfect. High gas fees during peak usage were a real problem. That's when Diego stumbled across Solana. He downloaded a wallet, tried a test transaction, and was shocked by the speed and cost—less than a penny and settled in seconds. He researched its proof-of-history consensus and how it allowed for such high throughput. Solana, he decided, was a bet on scalability. Riskier than Ethereum, sure, but potentially a critical piece of blockchain's mass adoption.

In the coming weeks, Diego explored more coins. Chainlink fascinated him—not because it was hyped, but because of its function. It served as a bridge between real-world data and smart contracts. He imagined a decentralized insurance app that automatically paid out after a natural disaster, using weather data fed through Chainlink oracles. It wasn't the sexiest use case, but it was essential. The infrastructure layer. Chainlink, he wrote in his journal, was the unsung hero of automation.

Then came Polygon. He had used a few Ethereum dApps and experienced the pain of $50 gas fees. Polygon offered an elegant solution—faster, cheaper transactions that still benefited from Ethereum's security. He liked that it wasn't trying to replace Ethereum, but to scale it. He joined Polygon's Discord, followed a few developers, and watched as projects began migrating or launching in parallel. This, he thought, was how real adoption would happen—not through revolutions, but through enhancements.

As he built his portfolio, Diego applied filters: Does this project solve a real problem? Is there a team behind it with a track record? Does it have actual users and developers? Is the tokenomics model sustainable? He passed on flashy meme coins and short-term pumps. He focused on projects that had been through a bear market and still stood. Resilience, he noted, was often the best metric of value.

He also kept track of Cardano, Avalanche, and Cosmos—each with its own vision and unique contributions. Cardano's research-heavy, methodical approach intrigued him. Avalanche's speed and low-latency smart contracts were promising. Cosmos, with its goal of making blockchains interoperable, seemed like the missing link in a fragmented industry. Diego didn't dive deep into all of them at once, but he bookmarked them for later, choosing to learn slowly and deliberately.

Eventually, Diego built a diverse portfolio—Bitcoin, Ethereum, Solana, Chainlink, and Polygon forming the core. But more importantly, he built conviction. When prices dropped, he didn't panic. He understood what he held. He understood why. He didn't need constant reassurance because his foundation was research, not hype.

One afternoon, a friend visiting Lisbon asked him if crypto was just a fad. Diego smiled. He pulled out his journal and flipped to the page that read, "Crypto: What's Real and What's Noise." He said, "It's not about chasing the next moonshot. It's about owning a piece of the future—responsibly, intelligently, and patiently."

That night, Diego walked the cobblestone streets of the city, headphones in, listening to another podcast. But now, he listened differently—not to be convinced, but to be informed. He was no longer a tourist in crypto. He was an investor.

Chapter 4: Building Your First Crypto Portfolio — Allocations, Tools, and Timing

Creating your first crypto portfolio is an exciting step in your investment journey. But it's also where many beginners make their biggest mistakes. Without a strategy, it's easy to chase hype, overexpose yourself to risk, or end up with a scattered collection of coins that lack cohesion. A well-structured portfolio reflects your goals, risk tolerance, and investment timeline. It balances growth potential with stability and gives you a framework for making smart decisions—even during market volatility.

The first step is choosing your **allocation strategy**. This means deciding how much of your portfolio will go into different categories of cryptocurrencies—such as large-cap, mid-cap, small-cap, and stablecoins. A beginner-friendly starting point could look like this:

- **60% in large-cap coins** like Bitcoin and Ethereum. These are the most established, most liquid, and most widely adopted assets in crypto. They should form the backbone of your portfolio.
- **25% in mid-cap coins** like Solana, Chainlink, or

Polygon. These projects have strong fundamentals and growth potential but are slightly riskier.

- **10% in high-risk, high-reward small-cap coins**, often newer projects that could explode in value—or crash.

- **5% in stablecoins** like USDC or USDT, which are pegged to the U.S. dollar. These can act as dry powder for buying dips or earning yield in DeFi platforms.

Of course, this is just a sample framework. You can tweak it based on your own goals. If you're very risk-averse, you might put 80% into Bitcoin and Ethereum. If you're more aggressive, you may increase your small-cap exposure. What matters is that you *define* a structure and stick to it—don't let emotions or market hype constantly reshape your allocation.

Next, let's talk about **investment timing**. One of the most powerful yet overlooked strategies is *dollar-cost averaging (DCA)*. Instead of trying to time the market, you invest a fixed amount of money at regular intervals—say $50 every week. This smooths out volatility over time, lowers your average entry price, and removes emotion from your decision-making. If prices drop, you buy more. If they rise, you still accumulate—slow and steady. This strategy is perfect for beginners and has historically outperformed lump-sum investments for volatile assets.

Now let's cover **essential tools** you need to manage your crypto portfolio:

1. **Wallets** – Use a combination of hot wallets (mobile apps like MetaMask or Trust Wallet) and cold wallets (hardware wallets like Ledger or Trezor) to balance convenience with security. Hot wallets are great for daily use and DeFi access. Cold wallets are ideal for storing long-term holdings safely offline.

2. **Exchanges** – Stick with reputable centralized exchanges like Coinbase, Kraken, or Binance for buying crypto with fiat. For decentralization and DeFi, learn to use platforms like Uniswap, SushiSwap, or PancakeSwap. Always verify URLs and enable two-factor authentication.

3. **Portfolio trackers** – Use apps like CoinStats, CoinGecko, Delta, or Blockfolio to monitor your holdings and track performance over time. Some tools allow you to connect wallets and exchanges for real-time updates.

4. **Security tools** – Use password managers, avoid public Wi-Fi when logging in, and consider using a

dedicated device for your crypto activity. Back up your seed phrases offline and never store them on cloud storage or email.

5. **Research tools** — Learn to use sites like CoinMarketCap, Messari, Token Terminal, and IntoTheBlock for data-driven insights. Follow credible crypto YouTube channels, podcasts, and Twitter threads to stay informed.

One important but often neglected step is to set clear **exit strategies**. At what point will you take profits? Will you sell 20% of your holdings when a coin triples in value? Will you rebalance your portfolio every quarter? Planning ahead helps prevent emotional decisions during parabolic price increases or sharp crashes.

Also, consider your **investment horizon**. If you're investing with a 5–10 year view, don't panic over short-term volatility. Let compounding work for you. But also remember that crypto changes fast. Reevaluate your positions every 3–6 months and stay flexible enough to adapt to major developments—like protocol upgrades, regulatory changes, or emerging trends.

Lastly, keep a journal. Document your strategy, entries, exits, lessons learned, and emotional reactions. It's one of the most valuable tools you'll ever use as an investor. You'll be amazed how much your thinking evolves—and how much better your decisions become when you track them.

In the next chapter, we'll dive into how to store and secure your crypto assets safely—because it doesn't matter how much you gain if you can't keep it secure.

How Malik invested intelligently in crypto

Malik had always been good with spreadsheets. As a freelance designer and part-time music producer, he tracked every client payment, expense, and royalty down to the penny. But when it came to investing, he always felt like an outsider. Stocks were too slow. Real estate seemed out of reach. And crypto? Well, that felt like a casino—until recently.

A friend had explained how crypto wasn't just speculation. It could be approached with structure, intention, and tools. That conversation stayed with Malik. One rainy weekend, he opened his laptop, brewed some tea, and decided it was time to build his first crypto portfolio—not to chase a moonshot, but to create a system.

He started with allocation. Malik didn't want to overthink it, so he modeled his first portfolio after a plan he'd read online: 60% Bitcoin and Ethereum, 25% strong mid-cap coins, 10% in new projects he was curious about, and 5% kept in USDC. It felt balanced, like an ecosystem—not just a bag of random bets. Bitcoin gave him peace of mind, Ethereum felt like investing in the future, and the rest gave him room to explore and learn.

To manage risk, he didn't go all in at once. Malik set a recurring buy order—$100 per week, divided across his picks. It was simple, but powerful. Every Monday, his exchange would automatically purchase coins and send a notification. He wasn't trying to time the market; he was building habits, discipline, and a slow-growing position in something bigger than himself.

As his portfolio took shape, he discovered the importance of tools. He downloaded Trust Wallet for quick access and exploration, but also ordered a Ledger Nano X to store his long-term holdings safely. He watched YouTube tutorials on how to transfer coins from exchange to cold storage. The first time he moved ETH to his Ledger, it felt like sending a message across the galaxy—and arriving safely.

He also explored CoinGecko to research coins, check charts, and read community comments. It became his daily routine: morning coffee, check his tracker, scan the news, then move on. He wasn't obsessed—just engaged. With Delta as his portfolio tracker, he had a clean dashboard that showed his holdings, profits, and market moves. It gave him clarity without emotional overload.

Then came a test.

One of the altcoins Malik had researched—an up-and-coming DeFi project—doubled in price over three days. Social media exploded. People were bragging about 10x returns. He felt the rush. But he paused and opened his notes. He had written a rule: "If something gains more than 100%, take profits on at least 20%." He followed it. Sold a piece. Transferred the stablecoins to USDC. The price crashed two days later. Malik felt a strange joy—not because he timed it perfectly, but because he *followed his plan.*

Over the next few months, he refined his portfolio. Some coins were swapped out. Others grew stronger. He created a spreadsheet to log every buy and sell with notes like, "Bought during a dip," or "Felt too emotional—waited a day." It was more than a tracker. It was a reflection of his growth as an investor.

Malik also started helping friends. He wasn't a guru, but he was thoughtful. He told them: "Start small. Use automation. Stick to a plan. Use tools. And don't invest in anything you don't understand." He hosted casual Sunday Zoom calls with friends to explain wallets, safety, and DCA. One friend said, "You made this feel human, not scary."

That was the moment Malik realized investing wasn't just about money. It was about learning to make decisions under uncertainty. About building systems when the world felt chaotic. About designing your future with the same care you'd put into a beat or a design mockup.

Malik still checked the markets, but he no longer stressed about every dip. He had a portfolio that reflected *him*—balanced, creative, organized, and long-term focused. And as he sat back one evening watching his tracker update, he thought: "This isn't gambling. This is building."

Chapter 5: Storing and Securing Your Crypto — Wallets, Keys, and Safety Practices

Once you've bought your first cryptocurrencies, the most important decision you'll make isn't *what* to buy—it's *how to store it safely.* The crypto world operates differently than traditional banking or investing. You are your own bank, which means you are responsible for securing your funds. If you lose your wallet keys, click a phishing link, or leave assets on a vulnerable exchange, no one can recover your funds. Understanding wallets, keys, and safety practices is essential to being a responsible investor.

To start, there are two main types of crypto wallets: **hot wallets** and **cold wallets**.

Hot wallets are connected to the internet. They're convenient, easy to use, and perfect for beginners or frequent transactions. Examples include mobile wallets like Trust Wallet, MetaMask, and Coinbase Wallet. These apps allow you to store, send, and receive crypto. However, since they are online, they are more vulnerable to hacks, malware, or phishing attempts. Think of them like the cash in your pocket—easy access, but not meant for holding your life savings.

Cold wallets, on the other hand, are offline. These include hardware wallets like Ledger Nano X, Ledger Nano S Plus, and Trezor. When you use a cold wallet, your private keys never touch the internet. This dramatically increases your security. Cold wallets are ideal for storing long-term holdings or large amounts of crypto. If you're serious about protecting your investment, owning a cold wallet is non-negotiable.

Every wallet comes with a **private key** or a **seed phrase** (usually 12–24 words). This is the most critical piece of your security. Your seed phrase is your master key—it gives full access to your funds. Anyone who has it can empty your wallet, and if you lose it, there's no way to recover your assets. Never store your seed phrase on your computer, phone, or cloud storage. Write it down on paper and store it somewhere fireproof and waterproof—ideally in a safe. Some people use metal seed phrase backup kits that resist fire and physical damage.

Next, let's talk about **custodial vs. non-custodial wallets**. When you keep your crypto on an exchange like Coinbase, Binance, or Kraken, you're using a *custodial wallet*. That means the exchange holds your private keys. It's convenient, but not fully under your control. If the exchange gets hacked, pauses withdrawals, or goes bankrupt (as seen with Mt. Gox or FTX), your assets could be frozen or lost. The rule is simple: **Not your keys, not your coins**.

By contrast, non-custodial wallets—like MetaMask or a hardware wallet—give you full control. You own your keys, and therefore you own your crypto. This control comes with responsibility, which is why beginners should start with small amounts until they're confident in managing non-custodial wallets securely.

Here are key **best practices for crypto security**:

- Enable **2FA (two-factor authentication)** on all accounts—especially exchanges and wallets.
- Never click on links or email attachments from unknown or suspicious sources. Phishing is one of the most common causes of wallet hacks.
- Always double-check URLs before logging in. Use bookmarks for exchanges to avoid fake websites.
- Use a **password manager** and create long, unique passwords for each crypto platform.

- Never share your seed phrase—not even with "support staff" or people claiming to help you recover lost funds.
- Consider using a **dedicated device** (or browser profile) for crypto activity only.
- Be careful with browser extensions—they can be hijacked or exploited by malicious code.

Also consider **multi-signature wallets** or **vaults** for even higher security. These wallets require multiple keys or approvals to move funds, which adds a layer of protection for joint accounts or large holdings.

Even in Web3 and DeFi, where you interact with smart contracts and dApps, wallet permissions can be risky. Always **review and revoke token approvals** regularly using tools like Etherscan's Token Approval Checker. Some malicious contracts can gain unlimited access to your tokens.

Lastly, **test everything** before committing large amounts. If you're transferring crypto to a new wallet or from an exchange to cold storage, do a small test transaction first. Verify that it arrives safely, then proceed with the full amount. And log everything—dates, amounts, destinations, and notes. A clear personal record can be a lifesaver in emergencies.

In summary, storing crypto securely isn't just a

precaution—it's a necessity. With great freedom comes great responsibility. When you control your assets, you also control your future. Don't leave it vulnerable to simple mistakes.

In the next chapter, we'll explore crypto investing strategies—how to identify opportunities, manage market cycles, and grow your portfolio intelligently.

Sophie's MetaMask story

Sophia had always considered herself tech-savvy. She'd been working in IT support for years, helping companies protect their data, secure their servers, and train staff on digital safety. But when she bought her first batch of crypto, she realized something important: securing *your own* money is different from securing someone else's data. It felt personal. And for the first time, it felt risky.

She had purchased Ethereum and Solana on a popular exchange and left them there, thinking that was enough. But a few days later, she read about an exchange hack that drained millions in customer funds. She froze. She imagined logging in and seeing a balance of zero. It was the kind of moment that changes your habits. That night, she committed to learning how to store her assets the *right* way.

Sophia started by researching wallets. She downloaded MetaMask, curious about how a non-custodial wallet worked. Setting it up took minutes, but the moment she saw her seed phrase—those 12 random words—she felt the weight of responsibility settle on her shoulders. It wasn't just a password. It was *everything*. She wrote it down on two separate sheets, storing one in her desk and the other in a waterproof envelope hidden in her closet. That seed phrase became the key to her freedom—and her vulnerability.

Wanting more security, she ordered a Ledger Nano X. When it arrived, it felt like a vault in the palm of her hand. Transferring funds to it was nerve-wracking at first. She sent a small test transaction—$20 worth of ETH—just to make sure she was doing it right. When it arrived safely, she breathed out and transferred the rest. Watching it disappear from the exchange and reappear on her cold wallet was empowering. She was now her own bank.

Her next step was to secure her digital environment. She created a fresh email address used only for crypto accounts. She enabled two-factor authentication everywhere—using an authentication app, not SMS. She set up a new browser profile dedicated only to crypto and disabled all extensions. She even created a separate user on her laptop with restricted access and encrypted storage.

But even with all these precautions, Sophia knew that human error was the real threat. So she practiced. She rehearsed what she'd do if her laptop was stolen, if her Ledger was lost, if her seed phrase was exposed. She wrote down a simple, step-by-step recovery process and stored it with her estate documents—just in case. Crypto wasn't just a tech hobby anymore. It was wealth, and wealth had to be protected.

She also helped her younger brother set up his wallet. He was new to the space and had almost fallen for a phishing scam that mimicked a support site. Sophia sat him down and walked him through the golden rules: *Never share your seed phrase. Always verify URLs. Bookmark your exchange login. Never trust random DMs*. It wasn't paranoia. It was preparedness.

As her portfolio grew, she began exploring DeFi, where she interacted with smart contracts and connected her wallet to various apps. She learned to revoke token approvals regularly and used tools to monitor activity linked to her wallet. It became a ritual—just like updating antivirus or backing up data.

One night, while reading in bed, Sophia thought about how far she'd come. A few months earlier, she was trusting third parties with her money. Now, she had full control. But it wasn't just about tools—it was about *awareness*. She had developed a level of vigilance that spilled into other areas of her life. She updated her estate plan to include wallet instructions, started using password managers for everything, and educated her parents on digital hygiene.

Crypto had taught her more than she expected. It taught her that control is powerful, but it comes with responsibility. It taught her that security isn't something you set and forget—it's a mindset. And it taught her that the future of finance belongs to those who are willing to learn, adapt, and protect what they've earned.

Chapter 6: Investing Strategies: Timing the Market, HODLing, and Taking Profits

Investing in cryptocurrency without a strategy is like sailing without a compass—you might catch the wind, but you'll eventually drift off course. In the crypto world, where volatility is the norm and emotions run high, having a clear, tested approach is your best defense against making impulsive, costly mistakes. This chapter will explore three essential investing strategies every beginner should understand: market timing, long-term holding (HODLing), and taking profits.

Let's start with the idea of **timing the market**. The goal of timing is simple in theory: buy low and sell high. But in practice, it's incredibly difficult—even for professionals. Crypto markets are irrational, fast-moving, and largely driven by sentiment. There are bull runs when prices skyrocket and euphoria takes over, and there are bear markets where panic and doubt dominate. Trying to predict exact tops and bottoms can lead to analysis paralysis—or worse, buying high and selling low.

That said, it is possible to *observe* market cycles and make smarter decisions based on patterns. For example, Bitcoin and most of the crypto market tend to follow a four-year cycle linked to the Bitcoin halving event. Prices typically rise leading into a halving and peak about a year after. Recognizing this pattern doesn't guarantee success, but it can help inform your timing around entry and exit points. Still, the safest approach for most investors is not trying to time the market precisely, but instead **dollar-cost averaging (DCA)**—consistently investing small amounts regardless of market conditions to average out your entry price.

Now, let's talk about **HODLing**—a popular term in the crypto space that originated from a misspelled word ("hold") in a forum post and evolved into a full-on investing philosophy: *Hold On for Dear Life*. HODLing means committing to long-term investing regardless of short-term volatility. It's about understanding the value of your assets and believing in their long-term potential, even during 70% drawdowns or market crashes. Investors who held Bitcoin from $100 to $1,000 to $10,000 to $60,000 saw wild swings, but long-term conviction paid off.

HODLing works best when you:

- Invest in fundamentally strong projects.
- Have a long-term thesis about where the market is going.

- Don't need the money in the short term.
- Have already planned for market volatility emotionally and financially.

HODLing is powerful, but it doesn't mean you never sell. That's where the third strategy comes in: **taking profits**. Most beginners make the mistake of riding gains all the way up—and all the way back down. A good strategy includes predefined profit-taking rules. For example, you might sell 20–30% of a position when it 2x's or 3x's in value. This lets you recover your original investment and ride the rest risk-free. Or you might take profits in phases—at 100%, 200%, and 400% gains.

You should also consider **rebalancing**. If one asset in your portfolio becomes disproportionately large (say it grows to 50% of your holdings), you can sell a portion and reallocate to underperforming assets or stablecoins. This keeps your portfolio aligned with your goals and prevents overexposure to a single coin.

Profits can be taken into:

- **Stablecoins** like USDC to park in yield platforms or wait for buying opportunities.
- **Fiat** (cash) if you need liquidity or want to lock in gains.

- **Other coins** if you're rotating from an overvalued asset to an undervalued one.

It's also smart to track your **return on investment (ROI)** and set **personal goals**. For example, if your goal is to grow your portfolio by 300% over 5 years, you may take profits at key milestones to ensure you're locking in those gains. Use tools like spreadsheets or portfolio apps to track your cost basis, targets, and exits.

Finally, one of the most important concepts in strategy is **emotional discipline**. You can't execute a plan you don't believe in. Set your strategy before the emotions hit. Make rules and follow them—especially when the market is euphoric or panicking. Crypto is a game of conviction, not reaction.

In the next chapter, we'll explore advanced topics like staking, yield farming, and how to generate passive income with your crypto holdings while managing the associated risks.

Now, let's talk about Ethan

Ethan was never an impulsive guy. He'd built a modest but solid life as an engineer, priding himself on structure, spreadsheets, and systems that made sense. But when it came to investing in crypto, he quickly realized logic didn't always rule the day. Prices swung like a rollercoaster, people on social media made wild predictions, and news headlines could send a coin up 30% or down 50% in hours. His first few months were filled with confusion—until he stopped chasing the perfect moment and started building a strategy.

It began the day he watched a coin he'd been tracking for weeks suddenly pump 80% overnight. He hadn't bought it because he was "waiting for a dip." But the dip never came. Then he jumped into another coin that everyone online was hyping—only to watch it crash 60% days later. He realized he was caught between fear of missing out and fear of getting burned. It wasn't sustainable.

So Ethan did what he always did in uncertain situations: he made a framework. He pulled out a whiteboard and wrote three words: *Timing. HODLing. Profits.*

He started with timing. He read everything he could about market cycles, the Bitcoin halving, past bull runs, and macro trends. He saw patterns, not predictions. Instead of trying to buy the exact bottom or sell the exact top, he decided to dollar-cost average. Every Friday, without fail, he invested a set amount. Sometimes prices were up. Sometimes they were down. But over time, his entry price evened out, and his stress levels dropped.

Then came the HODLing phase. He chose a handful of projects—Bitcoin, Ethereum, Solana, and Chainlink—that he believed would still be around in ten years. He committed to holding them no matter what, viewing them as his long-term digital property. He even created a separate folder in his tracker labeled "HODL Vault"—coins he wouldn't touch, no matter the headlines.

When the next crash came, and prices tanked 40%, Ethan didn't panic. He didn't sell. He didn't check his portfolio obsessively. Instead, he made tea, went for a walk, and added to his long-term positions like it was a Black Friday sale. That calmness didn't come from being fearless—it came from being *prepared.*

But Ethan wasn't naïve. He knew it wasn't smart to *never* take profits. He remembered the story of a coworker who rode a coin from $1 to $20—then all the way back to $3. That wasn't discipline. That was denial. So Ethan made a plan: when any coin in his portfolio doubled, he'd take out 25%. If it tripled, another 25%. This way, he recovered his initial investment early and let the rest ride with the house's money.

When Solana hit one of his target points, he followed his plan. He didn't hesitate. He sold a portion, moved it into USDC, and later used it to buy a promising coin that had just dipped. It felt good—not because he "beat the market," but because he made a clear decision ahead of time and stuck to it.

Over time, he refined his strategy. He added automatic alerts when a coin hit a target price. He created a spreadsheet with color-coded cells: green for buy zones, yellow for caution, red for exit signals. It wasn't about trading daily—it was about responding thoughtfully, not emotionally. His portfolio started to reflect his principles.

He also started writing short journal entries after every buy or sell. "Why did I do this?" "Was it fear, greed, logic, or discipline?" Some entries were honest admissions: "Sold too early—feared it would crash." Others gave him confidence: "Held through a dip and added more. Trusting my research." Reviewing them gave him a mirror—and made him a smarter investor.

One day, a friend new to crypto asked him, "How do you know when to sell?" Ethan paused, then said, "You don't always know. That's why you make the decision *before* the moment comes. The plan saves you from yourself."

Crypto investing didn't make Ethan rich overnight. But it did give him something more valuable: a toolkit of patience, conviction, and clarity. As he watched markets rise and fall like tides, he felt steady. Not because he knew the future—but because he had learned how to navigate it.

Chapter 7: Staking, Yield Farming, and Earning Passive Income with Crypto

One of the most exciting parts of the crypto space is the ability to **earn passive income** on your holdings. Unlike traditional assets that may require property management or stock dividends tied to company decisions, crypto enables you to put your digital assets to work through **staking**, **yield farming**, **lending**, and other decentralized finance (DeFi) strategies. When used properly, these methods can help you grow your wealth without selling your coins—but they also come with risks you must understand.

Let's begin with **staking**, the most beginner-friendly way to earn passive income in crypto. Staking is the process of locking up your coins to help support the operations of a blockchain network—usually those that use a **Proof-of-Stake (PoS)** consensus mechanism, like Ethereum 2.0, Cardano (ADA), Solana (SOL), and Polkadot (DOT). In return, you receive staking rewards—like interest paid in the same token.

There are two primary ways to stake:

1. **Direct staking**, where you run your own validator node. This requires technical knowledge and often large minimum token amounts (e.g., 32 ETH for Ethereum).

2. **Delegated staking**, where you delegate your tokens to a validator through a wallet or exchange. This is simpler and suitable for most investors.

Staking through platforms like Coinbase, Kraken, Binance, or wallets like Exodus and Atomic Wallet allows users to earn between 4–10% annually, depending on the token. The rewards are typically paid out automatically and compounded over time.

Next, there's **yield farming**, which is a more advanced (and riskier) way to earn passive income. Yield farming involves lending your crypto into **liquidity pools** on decentralized platforms like Uniswap, PancakeSwap, Aave, or Curve. These pools facilitate decentralized trading and borrowing, and in return, liquidity providers (LPs) earn fees and additional token incentives.

For example, by providing equal values of ETH and USDC to a trading pair pool on Uniswap, you earn a percentage of all transaction fees generated by trades between those assets. Some platforms even reward you with native tokens like UNI or CAKE as a bonus.

However, **yield farming comes with significant risks**, especially for beginners:

- **Impermanent loss**, where your assets lose value compared to simply holding them.
- **Smart contract vulnerabilities**, where code bugs or exploits can drain a pool.
- **Rug pulls**, where shady developers abandon a project and take investor funds.
- **Volatility**, where token rewards crash in value before you can claim them.

A safer, entry-level strategy is **crypto lending**, where you lend your coins to borrowers through platforms like Nexo, BlockFi (historically), Aave, or Compound and receive fixed interest payments. These platforms match lenders with borrowers and often require the borrower to provide overcollateralized loans. While centralized lending platforms have failed in the past, decentralized ones provide more transparency—but you must still research them thoroughly.

When considering these income strategies, ask:

- How is the yield generated?
- Is the platform audited and reputable?

- What are the risks (price volatility, contract security, liquidity)?
- Is the reward worth the risk?

Always start small, use well-known platforms, and never lock up assets you can't afford to lose or can't access quickly in an emergency. Keep in mind that **staking is usually less risky than yield farming or lending**, but yields may be lower.

Finally, track everything. Use DeFi dashboards like **Zapper**, **DeBank**, or **APY.Vision** to monitor your positions, earned rewards, and exposure. Set calendar reminders to withdraw or rebalance if you're in fixed-term protocols.

Passive income in crypto is powerful, but only when you treat it as a business—not a gamble. Know what your money is doing, where it's going, and how to take control of it.

In the next chapter, we'll explore how to navigate crypto taxes, reporting, and compliance—because growing your wealth is only half the battle; protecting it legally is just as important.

Jasmine learns staking

Jasmine had always been fascinated by the idea of passive income. As a full-time teacher and single mom, her days were packed from morning until night. The thought of earning money while she slept—or graded homework—sounded like a dream. That's what first pulled her toward cryptocurrency. Not just the potential price growth, but the opportunity to *earn* while holding. She didn't want to trade or time the market. She wanted to build something that quietly worked in the background.

After buying her first few coins—mostly Ethereum and Cardano—she discovered the concept of staking. "Earn 5% while holding?" she thought. "That sounds like a high-yield savings account, but smarter." Curious, she opened her Exodus wallet and clicked on the staking tab. It showed a breakdown of how rewards worked, and with just a few clicks, she staked a portion of her ADA. Days later, she saw the first reward notification. It wasn't much—maybe a few cents—but it was exciting. Her crypto was *growing* without her lifting a finger.

That's when she went deeper. She learned about delegated staking and started researching validators, reading community forums, and even joined a Discord group for Solana stakers. The more she learned, the more she appreciated the structure. This wasn't gambling. It was like earning interest for helping run the network. She staked her Solana next, then her DOT. Slowly, she began to see her balances increase—not because of speculation, but because of participation.

But Jasmine wasn't content just staking. When she heard about **yield farming**, her curiosity ignited again. She read blog posts and watched tutorials on YouTube that explained how to provide liquidity on platforms like Uniswap or PancakeSwap. At first, it sounded confusing—trading pairs, liquidity pools, impermanent loss. It was a new language. But she didn't rush in. She practiced by simulating scenarios on DeFi dashboards and asking questions in forums.

Finally, she decided to test the waters with a small amount—$100 split between USDC and ETH in a stable trading pool. It worked. Every day, she earned a tiny portion of transaction fees and a bonus token. It wasn't massive, but it was real. She was *participating* in the financial ecosystem, not just watching from the sidelines.

Over time, she experimented with different platforms—Aave for lending DAI, Curve for stablecoin farming, even a short-term pool on Polygon. But she never chased high APYs without doing research. She learned to ask: "Where's the yield coming from? Is this sustainable? What are the risks?" When friends got burned by a rug pull on a shady farm promising 1,000% APY, she nodded knowingly. She had passed on that one. Her rule was clear: if it sounds too good to be true, it probably is.

She also took security seriously. She used hardware wallets for long-term assets, created a dedicated wallet just for DeFi interactions, and revoked token approvals weekly. She journaled her experiences—what worked, what didn't, how her strategies evolved. Her notes weren't just financial—they were emotional. "Felt nervous about new farm. Waited 24 hours. Good call." "Staked DOT. Rewards feel slow, but solid." These became her personal guidebook.

Jasmine's proudest moment came when her son asked what she was doing. She explained it simply: "Mom is helping secure the internet of the future—and earning a little money for it." His eyes lit up. That night, he asked if he could learn too.

Crypto didn't make Jasmine rich overnight. But it made her feel in control. She was earning, learning, and growing—even in the middle of her busy life. Her passive income wasn't life-changing yet—but it was *life-affirming*. It showed her that, with the right tools and a steady approach, she could build a financial engine powered by technology, not time.

Chapter 8: Crypto Taxes, Reporting, and Legal Basics

Understanding the tax and legal implications of your crypto investments is just as important as choosing the right coins. Unfortunately, many beginners ignore this topic—until they get an unexpected letter from the tax authority. Crypto may be decentralized, but tax laws are not. Whether you're earning, trading, staking, or simply holding, you must stay compliant to avoid costly penalties and ensure long-term success. This chapter will cover the essentials of crypto taxes, record-keeping, and basic legal guidelines to help you operate responsibly.

Let's begin with the basics: **crypto is taxable**. In most countries, including the U.S., UK, Canada, and many others, crypto is treated as **property**, not currency. That means every time you sell, trade, or use crypto to purchase goods and services, it creates a **taxable event**—similar to selling a stock. The difference between your purchase price (cost basis) and sale price is a capital gain (or loss).

Here are the most common **taxable events** in crypto:

- Selling crypto for fiat (e.g., selling BTC for USD)

- Trading one crypto for another (e.g., exchanging ETH for SOL)
- Spending crypto on goods or services
- Receiving crypto as income (e.g., through freelancing, staking rewards, or airdrops)

Non-taxable events typically include:

- Buying and holding crypto (no taxable event until you sell)
- Transferring crypto between your own wallets
- Moving assets between exchanges (as long as you still control them)

Now let's talk about **capital gains**. If you sell crypto for more than you paid for it, you incur a **capital gain**. If you sell at a loss, you can claim a **capital loss**. The **duration** you held the asset matters:

- **Short-term capital gains** apply if you held the asset for less than a year. These are usually taxed at your regular income tax rate.

- **Long-term capital gains** apply if you held for more than a year. These are often taxed at a lower, favorable rate.

Income taxes apply to crypto earned through:

- Staking rewards
- Yield farming and DeFi earnings
- Airdrops
- Getting paid in crypto for work

This income is typically taxed at its fair market value in your local currency at the time you received it.

Record-keeping is essential. You'll need to track:

- Dates of acquisition and sale
- The amount of crypto bought or sold
- The fiat value at the time of each transaction
- Fees paid
- Wallet addresses and exchange details

Luckily, there are tools to help you automate this process. Popular crypto tax software includes **Koinly, CoinTracker, TokenTax, ZenLedger, and Accointing**. These platforms allow you to connect wallets and exchanges to automatically generate tax reports.

If you're a U.S. resident, be aware of **IRS Form 8949 and Schedule D** (for capital gains) and **Schedule 1** (for income from airdrops or staking). The IRS now asks a yes/no question on the front page of your tax return about whether you engaged in any crypto activity during the year. Answering inaccurately is considered tax fraud.

For international users, check your country's specific crypto tax rules. While some countries like Portugal or El Salvador currently have crypto-friendly policies, others have introduced strict reporting requirements. In some places, **failure to report crypto income** is treated the same as failing to report fiat income—and penalties can be severe.

Here are some **best practices** to stay compliant:

- Use a separate email and record system for crypto activity.
- Track everything from day one—wallet addresses, cost basis, dates, and counterparties.

- Save receipts or confirmations for purchases and transfers.
- Review tax laws at least once per year or when moving to a new jurisdiction.
- Consult a crypto-savvy accountant or tax advisor, especially if you earn income from DeFi or NFTs.

Lastly, avoid common mistakes like:

- Assuming crypto is anonymous and untraceable (it's not).
- Thinking crypto-to-crypto trades are tax-free (they're not).
- Failing to report small earnings from staking, referrals, or yield farming.

Compliance may feel intimidating, but it becomes manageable with the right tools and habits. It's far better to stay organized and proactive than to be caught off guard later.

In the next chapter, we'll dive into how to spot scams, protect yourself from fraud, and avoid the most common mistakes that catch beginners off guard.

Marco's crypto tax surprise

Marco had always prided himself on being a rule-follower. A meticulous planner and spreadsheet enthusiast, he was the guy who filed his taxes early, calculated his expected refund to the cent, and even saved all his digital receipts. When he began investing in crypto, he approached it with the same methodical care. But the more he read, the more confused he became. Taxes in the crypto world weren't simple—they were a maze. And one wrong step could cost him.

It started when Marco sold a small portion of Ethereum he had bought two years earlier. The price had nearly quadrupled, and he thought it was time to take some profits. A few weeks later, he swapped some of his SOL for MATIC. He didn't think twice about it—after all, it was just "moving money around," right? That was until he came across a Reddit post that made his heart sink: "Every crypto-to-crypto trade is a taxable event."

Marco's stomach dropped. He had made dozens of swaps and trades in the past year, each with a potential tax implication. Worse, he had used three exchanges, a hardware wallet, and two hot wallets. His transactions were everywhere. That night, he stayed up researching crypto taxation, realizing he had vastly underestimated its complexity.

He learned that selling crypto for fiat created capital gains. Trading ETH for SOL? Same. Even staking rewards, which he thought of as passive interest, were considered income at the time of receipt. The deeper he dug, the more overwhelming it became. So, Marco did what he did best—he created a system.

He signed up for a crypto tax platform called Koinly and connected his wallets and exchange accounts. Within minutes, a detailed transaction history loaded, color-coded with gains, losses, income, and fees. It even calculated his cost basis and flagged suspicious activity, like when a swap lacked market data. Marco felt a wave of relief. It wasn't perfect, but it gave him a starting point.

Still, the surprises kept coming. His airdropped tokens? Taxable. His DeFi yield? Income. Even transferring assets between wallets required him to label transactions carefully, or the system would assume they were sales. He realized that while the blockchain never forgets, it also doesn't explain itself. Every transfer, every token swap, every minor stake had to be documented and labeled. It was like translating a silent language into government paperwork.

Determined not to make mistakes, Marco scheduled a call with a crypto-savvy tax accountant. Together, they reviewed his report, discussed long-term vs. short-term gains, and planned how to carry forward his losses from a failed NFT project. The accountant gave him one invaluable piece of advice: "You're not just managing wealth—you're managing responsibility. The IRS may not understand DeFi, but they'll understand failure to report."

From that point forward, Marco built good habits. He labeled each transaction at the time it occurred. He created a monthly snapshot of his portfolio and used a dedicated email and password manager for all crypto accounts. He even set calendar reminders to export his tax reports quarterly, not just at year-end. It wasn't fun—but it felt smart.

Marco shared his experience at a local crypto meetup. When someone joked about crypto being "the wild west," he smiled. "Only if you ride without a map," he said. He explained how to automate reports, track staking rewards, and use long-term holding to reduce tax liability. People asked questions, took notes, and thanked him. He hadn't just saved himself—he was helping others navigate the storm.

By the end of the year, Marco had filed his first full crypto tax return. It was detailed, compliant, and—most importantly—accurate. No stress. No surprises. Just clean records and peace of mind. He didn't regret the gains he made, and he certainly didn't regret paying taxes on them. In fact, he saw it as a badge of legitimacy. Crypto wasn't just a hobby anymore. It was an investment—and like all investments, it required discipline, knowledge, and responsibility.

Chapter 9: Avoiding Scams, Mistakes, and Emotional Investing Traps

The cryptocurrency space is full of opportunity–but it's also filled with traps. Scams, emotional triggers, and costly mistakes have wrecked countless beginners who jumped in too quickly or trusted the wrong people. To succeed in crypto, it's not enough to understand charts and coins–you must learn how to protect yourself from deception, misjudgment, and your own emotions. In this chapter, we'll explore how to avoid the most common pitfalls in the crypto world and how to develop the mindset of a resilient investor.

Let's start with **scams**, which come in many forms. The most common include:

- **Phishing scams** that trick you into giving away your private keys or seed phrases via fake websites, emails, or DMs.
- **Rug pulls**, where a project lures in investors and then the developers disappear with the funds.
- **Pump-and-dump schemes**, where a coin is artificially inflated by hype and then rapidly sold off, leaving buyers with losses.

- **Fake giveaways**, where scammers impersonate influencers or companies offering to "double your crypto"—if you send it to their wallet first.

- **Impersonators and fake support**, especially on Telegram, Discord, or Twitter, offering to help with a wallet or exchange issue but actually trying to steal from you.

To protect yourself:

- Never share your **seed phrase** or private keys—ever. No legit support team will ask for it.

- Bookmark the official websites of exchanges and wallets.

- Use **two-factor authentication (2FA)** everywhere.

- Avoid clicking suspicious links, especially in DMs.

- Research projects thoroughly—check the team, whitepaper, social presence, and smart contract audits.

- Use tools like **RugDoc, TokenSniffer, and Dextools** to evaluate new tokens and projects before investing.

Now let's look at **common beginner mistakes**:

- **Overtrading** and trying to time every market movement without a strategy.
- **FOMO investing**—buying coins just because they're trending or everyone else is talking about them.
- **Ignoring fees**, especially on Ethereum-based platforms, where gas costs can eat into profits.
- **Going all in on one coin** without diversifying or setting stop-losses.
- **Investing more than you can afford to lose**, especially without understanding the risks.

Emotional investing is a trap that hits even experienced traders. The two main culprits are **fear and greed**. Greed pushes people to chase unsustainable gains, ignore red flags, or double down on hype. Fear causes panic selling during crashes or holding onto bad investments just to avoid admitting a loss. The key is to recognize when emotions are driving your decisions and return to logic and planning.

Here's how to manage emotional traps:

- **Write down your strategy** before you invest. Include your entry and exit rules.

- Stick to a **dollar-cost averaging plan** rather than reacting to price swings.
- Take **profits incrementally**—you don't have to sell everything at once.
- Remember that **no one goes broke taking profits**—but many go broke chasing more.
- Zoom out. Crypto is volatile daily but trends upward over years.
- Follow your own plan, not the crowd.

Avoid the trap of **confirmation bias**, where you only seek opinions or content that support your investment decisions. Stay curious, but skeptical. Evaluate your portfolio with a critical eye and be willing to change your mind based on new facts—not emotions.

Lastly, understand the **influence of social media**. Twitter, TikTok, Discord, and Telegram are powerful tools—but also breeding grounds for misinformation, pumpers, and scammers. Take advice with a grain of salt, verify sources, and never make investment decisions based solely on influencer hype. Most serious investors spend more time reading whitepapers and following project updates than watching viral clips.

Surviving and thriving in crypto isn't about perfection. It's about avoiding the big mistakes, staying calm under pressure, and sticking to a process. Smart investing isn't emotional—it's intentional.

In the final chapter, we'll bring it all together and look at how to create a sustainable crypto wealth-building plan that fits your goals and lifestyle.

Lena's story

Lena was a fast learner, but even she had to admit—crypto had humbled her. She'd started with excitement, watching her small investment in Ethereum double, then triple within months. She felt like she had discovered a secret world of opportunity. Fueled by confidence, she joined several Telegram groups, followed flashy influencers, and poured more money into trending tokens. But it didn't take long for reality to check her ego.

The first red flag came with a project promising 10x returns in a week. The website looked sleek. The whitepaper used buzzwords she only half understood. Everyone in the chat group swore it was the next big thing. So she jumped in—$1,000 into a new token she'd never heard of the week before. Within 48 hours, the token dropped 80%. Then the website went offline. The Telegram group vanished. The devs deleted their profiles. Rug pull.

Lena was furious. But mostly, she was embarrassed. She hadn't done proper research. She had let hype override caution. Worse, she ignored her own instinct—the moment when she thought, "This feels too good to be true." That loss wasn't just financial. It stung her confidence.

Determined to learn from her mistake, Lena took a break. She unsubscribed from crypto Twitter, left all Discord groups, and spent two weeks reading security guides and listening to interviews with long-term investors. She learned about phishing scams, fake support messages, and how a single seed phrase leak could drain a wallet. She reviewed her own setup and realized she'd stored her recovery phrase in a cloud document—something she corrected immediately.

With renewed focus, she created a checklist for evaluating any new token: verify the development team, check audit status, confirm liquidity lock, examine tokenomics, and test community transparency. She never invested again without following her own rules.

But the hardest part wasn't avoiding scams—it was managing her own emotions.

When markets dipped, she felt panic. She checked prices constantly, her mood rising and falling with the charts. At one point, she considered selling all her holdings during a 30% crash. But instead, she opened her notes and re-read the reasons she invested in the first place. The long-term vision. The technology. The gradual adoption. She made herself a promise: "If I bought it for a reason, I'll only sell it for a better one."

She stopped trying to time the market and switched to dollar-cost averaging. Every Friday, she bought small amounts—no matter the price. She journaled her decisions. When she felt euphoric, she wrote, "You're not a genius, the market is just green." When she felt scared, she reminded herself: "Volatility is the cost of opportunity."

She also started taking profits—something she hadn't done before. When a coin doubled, she sold a portion and moved it into stablecoins. She didn't wait for the perfect top. She accepted good gains and protected her capital. It wasn't thrilling, but it was smart. Each time she took profit, she felt more in control.

Months passed. The market went through another cycle of hype, then fear. Friends texted her asking if they should buy "the next big coin." She asked them questions: "What does the project do? Who's the team? Is there an audit?" Most couldn't answer. She didn't try to convince them—she just shared her story and let them learn the way she had.

Lena's portfolio grew slowly, but steadily. More importantly, her *conviction* grew. She no longer felt like a spectator or a gambler. She was an investor—one who had been burned, bounced back, and built a system that worked.

Looking back, she wasn't ashamed of her early mistakes. They were part of the path. Every loss, every panic moment, every lesson helped shape the investor she became. She didn't need to win every trade. She just needed to stay in the game long enough for her smart decisions to compound.

And she did—quietly, patiently, confidently.

Chapter 10: Creating Your Long-Term Crypto Wealth Plan

Now that you understand the fundamentals of cryptocurrency investing—how to buy, store, grow, protect, and manage your assets—it's time to build something even more powerful: a long-term crypto wealth plan. The goal isn't just to make money. It's to create sustainable, life-changing wealth that supports your future. Whether you're starting with $100 or $100,000, this chapter will help you map out a clear, customized path based on your unique goals, lifestyle, and risk tolerance.

Start with a **vision**. What does financial freedom look like to you? For some, it means early retirement. For others, it might be paying off debt, funding travel, supporting family, or simply having more peace of mind. Define what you're working toward—not just a dollar amount, but a feeling, a lifestyle, a timeline. This clarity will guide every decision you make in crypto and keep you from chasing noise.

Then, build your **crypto core portfolio**. By now, you've learned how to diversify across large-cap coins like Bitcoin and Ethereum, mid-cap projects like Solana and Chainlink, and emerging tokens. But your long-term plan needs consistency.

Allocate your holdings with purpose. For example, your core portfolio might be:

- 60% in long-term holds (BTC, ETH)
- 25% in growth projects
- 10% in staking/yield platforms
- 5% in stablecoins for flexibility and emergencies

Update your portfolio quarterly, but avoid over-trading. Rebalance only when an asset drifts significantly from your planned allocation.

Establish a **wealth-building strategy**. Are you adding a fixed amount each month? Are you reinvesting staking rewards? Are you taking profits and converting them into income-producing assets like real estate or dividend stocks? Don't let crypto gains sit idle—have a plan for compounding them or protecting them.

Consider **exit strategies**. Crypto markets are volatile, and major bull runs don't last forever. Plan when you'll take profits, how much you'll cash out, and where you'll move those funds. You could:

- Convert profits into fiat and set them aside in savings

- Roll gains into stablecoins to earn passive income
- Reallocate into lower-risk assets
- Fund other goals like a house, education, or retirement

A good rule is to take partial profits at predetermined milestones—don't try to sell everything at the top. Taking chips off the table along the way protects you from losing everything in a crash.

Your plan should also include **risk management**. Set limits on how much of your net worth goes into crypto. Diversify beyond crypto into other asset classes over time. Keep emergency funds outside of your crypto wallets. Think of crypto as one powerful engine of your wealth plan—not the whole vehicle.

Don't forget **tax planning**. Know how your country treats long-term gains, staking rewards, and DeFi earnings. Use crypto tax software year-round, not just at filing time. If your portfolio grows large, consider working with a tax advisor familiar with digital assets.

Also, take **estate planning** seriously. If something happens to you, will your family know how to access your wallets? Where are your seed phrases stored? Have you left clear instructions in a will or digital legacy plan? Crypto inheritance isn't automatic–if you don't plan, your assets could be lost forever.

Now bring it all together in a **Crypto Wealth Blueprint**. This is your one-page summary that outlines:

- Your purpose for investing
- Portfolio allocation and assets
- Investment schedule and DCA plan
- Passive income strategies
- Exit points and profit targets
- Security, storage, and seed phrase management
- Tax and estate plan reminders

Keep it updated. Review it quarterly. And most importantly–follow it. A written plan removes emotion from decisions and keeps you grounded through bull runs and bear markets.

Finally, adopt a **wealth mindset**. Stay patient. Think long-term. Focus on skills, not just gains. Keep learning–about crypto, economics, finance, and yourself. The market will test your resolve many times. But those who stay consistent, humble, and prepared will be the ones who win—not just financially, but in confidence, freedom, and peace of mind.

In the next and final section, we'll close this book with a powerful reflection and roadmap in the **Epilogue**—your personal launchpad for long-term success in the digital economy.

Now, let's go over Raj's "Crypto Wealth Blueprint" story

Raj had always been a long-term thinker. As a mechanical engineer, he was used to planning years ahead, building systems that had to function flawlessly over time. So when he began investing in crypto, he didn't want a quick hit. He wanted a blueprint—something he could follow, measure, and improve. For him, crypto wasn't about fast cars or viral coins. It was about designing financial independence.

His journey started modestly—a few hundred dollars spread across Bitcoin and Ethereum. But once he saw the potential of staking, yield, and strategic timing, he knew he needed more than scattered moves. He needed a plan. One Saturday morning, Raj opened a fresh notebook, titled the first page *"Crypto Wealth Blueprint,"* and started mapping.

First came the **vision**. Raj wasn't aiming for yachts or luxury. What he really wanted was freedom: the ability to step away from corporate life in a decade, move back closer to family, and work on personal projects without worrying about money. His target? Build a $500,000 crypto portfolio by the time he turned 45. It felt ambitious—but clear.

Then came the **structure**. He divided his portfolio into buckets:

- 60% in long-term holds—Bitcoin, Ethereum, and a little Solana.
- 20% in emerging tech tokens—AI, interoperability, and privacy projects.
- 10% in staking—rewards rolled automatically back into his holdings.
- 5% in stablecoins as his buffer.
- 5% in a "wild card" fund for new experiments, fully accepting those might fail.

He printed this allocation and taped it near his desk—not to limit himself, but to stay disciplined.

Every two weeks, Raj invested a fixed amount, using dollar-cost averaging. He tracked his buys and portfolio performance in a spreadsheet, noting price, timing, and reason for entry. When a token doubled, he took 25% profits and moved them into either USDC or long-term projects. When a token underperformed, he re-evaluated—not emotionally, but based on utility, adoption, and roadmap updates.

He created a **compounding system**. His staking rewards went right back into the asset. His stablecoins earned yield in low-risk DeFi protocols. When profits were strong, he rebalanced—occasionally moving excess into a traditional brokerage account for stock dividends or even setting aside cash for real estate.

But he also planned **exit strategies**. He didn't want to be the investor who rode a bull run to the moon, then watched it crash back to Earth. So he set milestones: take partial profits at 2x, 3x, and 5x gains. Roll 10% of each milestone into cash, 10% into stablecoins, and use the rest strategically. It wasn't about timing the top. It was about *harvesting gains without regret.*

Raj also built a **security and succession plan**. He stored seed phrases offline, split across two cities. He gave his sister instructions on accessing his wallets, included crypto in his will, and kept a printed "crypto key map" in a sealed envelope. He didn't see it as paranoia—he saw it as responsibility.

Then came tax season. He was ready. Using CoinTracker, he exported every transaction. His categories were clean: income, capital gains, transfers. He sent everything to his accountant, who called him saying, "Most people don't even know where their crypto is. You could teach a course."

Perhaps one day, Raj thought.

Over the next year, he reviewed his blueprint quarterly. He tweaked strategies, added a new passive income layer with DeFi loans, and removed one underperforming token. But his core stayed solid. He wasn't gambling. He was growing.

One evening, sitting on his balcony, sipping chai, he looked over his updated crypto plan. He wasn't "rich," but he was *wealthier*—in clarity, discipline, and direction. He wasn't chasing trends. He was building freedom.

And with every smart decision, every page filled in his blueprint, he was designing the life he had always envisioned—one trade, one plan, one quiet win at a time.

Epilogue: Your Journey Begins Now

You've come a long way. From the fundamentals of Bitcoin and Ethereum to wallets, security, portfolio planning, and passive income—this book has walked you through the core pillars of crypto investing. And while the learning will never stop, you've built a foundation that many people will never take the time to establish. That puts you in a unique position: you're not just a participant in this space—you're prepared to thrive in it.

But let's be honest—crypto is not an easy path. The markets are volatile. The rules evolve. The noise is constant. There will be days when you doubt everything, and other days when you feel invincible. But remember this: long-term wealth isn't built by being right all the time. It's built by showing up consistently, learning from your mistakes, and staying focused when others lose their way.

The people who succeed in crypto aren't necessarily the smartest or most technical. They're the ones who approach this journey with intention. They protect their assets. They follow a plan. They invest in learning, not just earning. And when they win, they do so quietly—not because they got lucky, but because they were prepared.

If there's one truth that defines the crypto space, it's this: **we're still early**. Blockchain technology is still evolving.

Regulation is still taking shape. Global adoption is still accelerating. That means you have time—time to build, to position yourself, and to grow as the world catches up. But it also means that every decision you make today has the power to compound into something life-changing tomorrow.

So what should you do next?

- Revisit your goals. Are they still relevant? Do they reflect your values, your timeline, and your risk tolerance?

- Tighten your security. Back up your seed phrases. Review wallet permissions. Audit your processes.

- Optimize your portfolio. Is it balanced? Are your allocations aligned with your convictions?

- Keep learning. Follow credible sources. Explore new protocols. Understand what's behind the projects you invest in.

- Educate others. Whether it's a friend, a parent, or a coworker—sharing what you've learned helps you deepen your understanding and strengthen your conviction.

- Stay grounded. Take breaks from the noise. Focus on

what you can control. And never let short-term hype derail long-term discipline.

If you're building wealth in crypto, you're doing more than making money. You're participating in a new financial era. An era where the tools of wealth-building aren't locked behind legacy systems or limited to the few. You're taking responsibility. You're creating independence. And you're becoming part of a community that believes in transparency, decentralization, and opportunity for all.

You may still feel like a beginner. That's okay. The best investors never stop being students. But if you've made it this far, you've already done something most people never will: **you took action**.

And from here, it's no longer about watching what happens next. It's about shaping it—with intention, with patience, and with the knowledge that the journey you've started could change everything.

Your crypto future begins now. Go build it.

www.ingramcontent.com/pod-product-compliance
Lightning Source LLC
LaVergne TN
LVHW022016200926
848481LV00007B/2416
* 9 7 9 8 3 4 9 6 4 4 5 3 5 *